Truckin Secrets

THE THINGS THEY DON'T TELL YA!

BRUCE DANGELO

Fulton Books
Meadville, PA

Published by Fulton Books 2022

ISBN 979-8-88505-531-4 (paperback)
ISBN 979-8-88505-532-1 (digital)

Printed in the United States of America

This idea came to me while I was sitting in a snowstorm in a truck stop in Grand Junction, Colorado, USA.

I'm getting close to retirement age, and I see the young drivers, and I remember how it was to learn all the things they don't teach you in truck driving school. This guide should help people with a lot of those problems. I wrote this guide for active drivers, new drivers, and folks who just wonder how this lifestyle works.

Good luck and keep on trucking!

CONTENTS

CHAPTER 1

YOU

You are the most important piece of this whole puzzle. Truckers come in all shapes, sizes, colors, and genders. You will be meeting a lot of interesting people. Keep an open mind when you are on the job. Enjoy yourself, but always stay alert. Stay well rested; only do as much as your body will allow you to do.

Don't Be a Hero!

Keep yourself in good shape. It's very easy to let yourself go being a truck driver. This is a very different way of making a living. You don't work a typical Monday through Friday week. You work what's needed to get your work done. There are times when it gets pretty tough no matter how long you have been a driver.

That's why I personally like trucking. I like the challenge. There will be plenty of challenges.

You should keep yourself clean. Shower as much as possible. This is very important. Stay active, take walks, exercise, and anything you can do to stay active. There are days when just shutting the truck down and jumping in your bunk is all you want to do. I totally understand that, and that is totally fine, but when you can get away from the truck, go for it.

Sometimes I will pull over and snap a few pictures of where I am at just for fun. It makes you understand how special of a job you have. You wouldn't be taking too many pictures if you worked at a factory!

Enjoy the Ride!

Eat right! Try to stay out of the fast-food lines. Buy a microwave oven. Very good investment. Quick tip when you are using your microwave oven, keep your truck running while you are cooking. They can be hard on your truck batteries. If you have a refrigerator, fill it up. Remember, *ticktock!* Every time you stop for any reason, that's at least a half-hour of your time clock. It takes time to park the truck, go into the store, order food, and do whatever else is needed. It all adds up. When I'm off and at home, I like to cook. I make a lot of pasta dishes, beef dishes, and chicken dishes. I always make enough to take food out on the road when I take it back out. This is a great way to eat well and save a bunch of money. Your biggest expense will be food. Whatever you can do to save money will help you big time.

The bottom line is to take care of yourself. Lots of people try truck driving but fail because they can't handle the job. They quit for all sorts of reasons. It's a marathon, not a sprint. It's very hard to be on the road for long periods of time. It's more of a lifestyle than a job!

Good luck!

CHAPTER 2

YOUR TRACTOR

The second most important piece of this puzzle is your tractor. When you get your tractor friend, take that manual and go through it cover to cover. This is your partner, and you have to understand what it can and can't do.

Learn what every button on that dashboard is for because you will use them all sooner or later. Buddy up with another driver from your company so if you do have troubles, you can call them for some help.

Keep your truck clean. This is your home when you're not home. Wipe that tractor down inside as much as possible. Most companies will let you wash your truck once a month. The winter months are rough on trucks. Keep it clean!

Carry a gallon of the correct oil and antifreeze with you at all times. Carry a spare headlight, wiper blades, fuses, glad hand seals, windshield wash, big funnel, rags, and grease for your fifth wheel.

Grease on your fifth wheel is extremely important. Trucks love to eat grease. You should be greasing your fifth wheel at least once a week.

They sell it at the truck stops in bottles or individual plastic packets. When you grease your fifth wheel, put two packets on the wheel. One on each side in the middle. If you go with the bottle, just layer it on the wheel. On your dashboard, you should have a button or switch to let your airbags deflate. Deflate your bags, then back under your trailer so the plate is under the trailer. Reinflate your airbags, then hook up to your trailer. Make sure you have a good tight hookup. If you just grease the plate and slide under the trailer, most of your grease will end up on the ground.

Checking your oil. A diesel engine is designed differently than a gasoline engine. When you shut down a diesel engine, it takes about twenty minutes for all the oil to drain back into the oil pan. This is why I always check my oil before I start my day. That way, you will have an accurate reading on the dipstick. That's the time to check all your fluids. The truck should also be on level ground.

Most companies will let their drivers wash their trucks at least once a month. Take advantage of that, especially in the winter months. Snow and ice are very hard on a tractor. Keep it clean. Take pride in your ride!

CHAPTER 3

YOUR DISPATCHER

Dispatchers are very interesting people. They are usually in a hurry because they are multitasking. When you talk to them, it probably will be short and sweet. What a driver must know is that a dispatcher can make you or break you. No matter what type of personality your dispatcher may have, it is extremely important that you both get along with each other. You must form a bond of trust with that person as soon as possible.

That all starts with you. They have to know that when they give you a load, you can get the load from point A to point B on time. Once that trust factor is established, then you will get better loads, and that means more money in your wallet. Things will get better for both of you once this bond is formed.

Communication is extremely important with your dispatcher. Truck drivers that do dedicated work have a route they stick to, so dispatch is fairly simple. Over the road, drivers have a very different lifestyle. Every day is a different situation. The dispatcher is a critical part of the puzzle. When things start going bad for any reason, reach out to your dispatcher. Don't assume things will get better because usually they don't. Keep in contact. Remember, you are doing the work here. If you don't let them know you're having troubles, they can't help you!

CHAPTER 4

TRUCK STOPS

Truck stops are what I like to call a necessary evil. I have been to just about every state in the United States. When it comes to truck stops, they are definitely not all the same. This is where keeping a journal of places to stay comes in mighty handy. Let's use the East Coast. It has fewer truck stops than the West Coast. They are smaller, harder to get in and out of; most of the time, very full, and for the most part, just plain trouble.

You can waste a lot of time in truck stops that are not even worth stopping at. Remember, *ticktock!* You need to learn about the bad truck stops and just stay out of them unless you absolutely have got to stop there.

Reasons not to stop would be, takes forever to get in and out, big potholes everywhere, hot spot for bad people, super dark at night, food is lousy, and whatever else you can think of. Don't waste your time, just keep rolling until you can get someplace decent. A lot of companies have repeat clients, and even though America is a large country, you get to know certain places. That being said, if you have some idea where to fuel, sleep, eat, and shower before you start your day, your day will be a lot better. That takes a lot of stress of you.

The fuel island is also a place to understand how life works. Everybody has got to stop for fuel. Everybody has also got their clocks ticking. There is nothing more irritating than getting to the fuel island and getting behind another truck and seeing no fueling going on. When you get to the fuel island, fuel your truck, clean your glass, and either move up or go park your truck. I'm noticing more and more drivers just don't seem to understand the concept of this whole procedure. It's a common-sense thing. Don't get to the fuel pumps and then go into the store for a half-hour. You won't have many friends when you come back to your truck. The bottom line is everybody is trying to make a living, and in this business, time is very important. If you have that mindset, you will have very few problems. Always be thinking ahead.

CHAPTER 5

THE ROAD AND ME

Where to start? Okay, so here you are on a nice fresh seventy-hour workweek, and you're thinking, *I got this covered.* Then three days go by, and just about everything that can go wrong does go wrong. Before you develop a bad attitude, please don't. Regroup a little bit. The good news is, a bad week is usually followed up by a good week. It sorts of evens itself out. When you're in this trucking world, some weeks are tough slugging. I always try to have a game plan on how the run will pan out. After being on the road, you will find out that half the time, that just doesn't happen. Being flexible is the key. If you get out of sorts, sometimes it's best to just shut it down and live to fight another day.

Travel days are great. You can just drive and enjoy. Days when you have to unload and load back up are not quite as fun. Get used to it because that's what this is all about. There will be times when you will sit for long periods of time while unloading and loading. It's the same problem for everybody, so don't think you are the unlucky one. Remember, it's a marathon, not a sprint. Just relax and start planning your next move.

Things that most definitely will happen to you while you're driving will be fatigue, cramps, and just getting sore in general. They call it hitting the wall. It happens to every driver sooner or later. When this starts to happen, pull that truck over somewhere safe and take a break. Get out and move around. Eat something, do anything to break the momentum. Even if it's five minutes, it will always help.

Don't Be a Hero!

Okay, so before you fire up that ELD (time clock) in the morning, you should do everything possible that you need to do so you don't waste your driver time. Things like personal functions, taking the dog out, getting coffee, wandering around the store, and training yourself to get up a bit earlier.

Remember, *Ticktock!*

Once you fire up your clock, it's game on, so use your time wisely. Make sure you are ready to roll when you roll. Nothing worse than getting on the big road and then realizing my coffee is behind me, or my phone is on the bed. Now you have to pull over and figure all that out. It's wasted time, and after a while, it all adds up.

When you get to your shipping or delivery customer, have all your information written down in a notebook. There are a few reasons for this. It's super easy to answer their questions. Things like pickup numbers, contacts, and destination. It's also nice to have this information in case, say, a week later, your dispatcher has a question about that load. The notebook comes in handy when your dispatcher doesn't have an exact address but tells you to start heading for the city you need to go to. You can pop an address in your GPS just to get you rolling. I will put it in plain sight when I'm getting close to my destination so I have all the information right in front of me.

You don't want to miss your shipping or receiving gate because then you have to find a place to turn around. This is a good time to make a driving mistake. It's also a major waste of time! Don't be that driver!

After I'm into my drive day, I always try to figure out where my day is going to end. Always think ahead. Again, having a journal is good. Buy a trucker's road guide. It will list a lot of places to sleep. They can be bought at all truck stops. When you find places you like to stay at, make sure you put them in your personal journal for future reference.

When you are not driving, try to stay out of the driver's seat. Your body is in that position all the time.

Go for a walk, exercise, and lie down. You need to give those muscles a rest. Anything that you can do will help you out big time. I get out of my truck as soon as I shut the truck down. I always take a quick walk around the truck. I'm doing my post-trip inspection, but more importantly, I'm getting my blood flowing to different parts of my body. Do whatever works for you, but definitely get out of the driver's seat.

Good luck!

CHAPTER 6

FATHER TIME

Father time is very important. When you first get on the road, it seems like things are moving way too fast. Seems like you are always fighting the clock. After a while, things will slow down for you as you get more comfortable with how things work. That pressure will always be there because that is the nature of this profession. It's not easy taking a load of freight from one side of the country to the other side and getting it there on time.

That being said, if you get good at it, you can make a lot of money!

You will have days when you don't do much driving, and it seems like you're just wasting your time, but it all evens out in the end. I personally like to start out early and get done early. That makes finding a place to park your truck a lot easier. The later into the day or night, your work makes it harder to find a spot to park your truck and rest. Keep this in mind, especially if you are on the East Coast.

I personally like to drive about a nine-hour day on travel days. This will keep your drive time fairly even. Everyone has their own formula for how long to drive in a day, but nine hours work well for me.

The trucker clock is very different from the forty-hour workweek clock. Here is a breakdown of how it works:

- Total hours—seventy hours a week

- On duty hours—fourteen hours a day
- Off duty hours—ten hours a day
- Drive time hours—eleven hours a day

You get fourteen hours a day to work. You may drive up eleven hours a day. Within your first eight hours, you must take a half-hour break. I try to drive about nine hours a day. That leaves me with enough time to park the truck because there are days when parking the truck takes some time due to where and what is going on. One example, it's late and dark, and you're in a strange place, and it's full, so you move on to someplace else. Now you are glad you have an extra hour of time because you are going to need it! This is when you get out your journal and trucker guide and go to plan B! My advice is start early and get done early!

Make sure you have enough time on your seventy-hour clock to get the load to where it has to go. If you're not sure, call your dispatcher. They will help you out with that situation.

Being an over-the-road driver means you definitely won't have a normal lifestyle. There will be times when your personal time clock will get turned upside down. It all depends on how long it takes to get your truck loaded, when is your delivery date, and the time is scheduled. This is very hard on a driver because the human body clock is not designed to work this way. All I can say is get as much rest as you can. Going from daytime driving to nighttime driving is hard. I know drivers who will not do night driving. I personally consider this part of my job.

Things totally change at night in a big truck. You have to slow your pace. Taking turns, dealing with on and off-ramps, and moving around in truck stops. These things all become a whole different world. At night, the animals are on the move. I like to drive with my bright lights on as much as possible. It freezes the animals most of the time. Make sure to turn your brights off when other drivers are coming your way! I myself do quite a bit of night driving. That being said, if you can become comfortable driving at night, you can make a lot of money.

Let's get back to the actual clock. Sometimes your seventy-hour clock will run out while you're out on the road. You can either do what they call a "reset." Reset means you park your truck someplace and sit for thirty-four hours. Option number two is you work off your previous week's hours. Working on your previous week's hours gets a little tricky because it depends on what you did the previous week. If you choose to do this, make sure you know what hours you have for actual drive time. Most folks just reset, then get a fresh seventy hours back on their clock. When you reset, make sure you park at a good place. Decent facilities, good food, etc. Thirty-four hours is a long time to sit in your truck.

Good luck!

CHAPTER 7

GENERAL TIPS

Let's talk about big cities. When I'm making a delivery to a big city, I like to stay fifty to seventy miles away. There are a few reasons for this. It's easier to park the truck for the night. I don't have to pay to park the truck. Examples: Houston, Tucson, East Coast cities, California, etc. You also will be a lot safer. Big cities are trouble. It's nice to get in, get unloaded, and get out.

When traveling through big cities, you always want to make sure your time situation is solid. Give yourself extra time for traffic, accidents, and whatever else is going on that day. Make sure your fuel tanks are at least half-full. Try to go through big cities very early in the morning or later in the evening.

I'm talking about New York City, Chicago, Dallas, Houston, Atlanta, Boston, Washington, DC, and Los Angeles. If you can avoid rush hour in the big cities, your job will be less stressful.

When making moves at your destination, always go slow. Have your flashers on. Try to get that truck where it's going on the first attempt. Then make your small moves to square it up.

If you have to spin around, make right-hand turns if possible. Going left can sometimes get you in trouble if you really get into a tight spot. You might pinch your lines and break a glad hand or wreck your electrical connection to your trailer.

Lane changes are another thing that can get you in trouble. You should know what your truck can and can't do.

Most tractors these days are running about 450 horsepower engines. The problem is some truckers (mainly owners/operators) are running tractors with six hundred or 650 horsepower. They get very unhappy with the 450-horsepower crowd when they are in the hammer lane (passing lane), and they are holding up the parade. Don't be that driver!

You need to understand that this is like dancing. Some trucks lead, and some trucks follow. Make sure you know which one you are! If you run out west, the speed limits are high, and the tempers are short.

Let's talk about engine brakes, also known as Jake Brakes. The engine brake is designed to retard the engine so that the driver can stay off the brake pedal. It will also keep your truck under control. Most trucks have engine brakes.

They usually have a low, medium, and high setting. Get to know your engine brake. I drove quad axle dump trucks for eight years. My engine brake was like my right arm. If you're running in the mountains, your engine brake is a must. I have mine on most of the time. When going down mountains or steep slopes, get that truck in the proper gear and get your engine brake on high and take your truck down at a speed you are comfortable with.

Stay off that brake pedal as much as possible. Let that engine brake do the work. Stab that brake pedal when you need to, but don't ride the brake pedal. Stab it, wait, stab it, wait; you want your air pressure to remain steady. If you ride your brake pedal, you're going to burn up your brakes, and you're going to lose your air pressure. You don't want either one of these things to happen. You can practice these moves on smaller hills so you get used to making them. Get to know what is the right gear to be in for a four-degree hill, five-degree hill, and six-degree hill. Practice makes perfect.

Keep a small notebook for good spots to sleep, eat, and shower. Go state by state, what highway, what exit, or town. If you record this information in your notebook before too long, you will have a nice journal. It's nice to have this to look at because you can flip it to the state you're currently driving in and get a quick idea of what your options are for parking your truck. Buy yourself a pocket truckers guide. This guide breaks out truck stops, rest areas, and small spots to stay state by state.

Between the trucker's guide and your journal, you will usually have a good idea of where to park your truck.

There is a phrase in the trucking world that every driver should know and understand. It's one word—GOAL. It means get out and look. If you're making any kind of move and things don't seem right, get out and look. This will be happening all the time. Better to be safe than sorry.

The GPS is a great tool, but they do get fooled sometimes. If it's telling you to do something that is not making sense, don't make that move; just keep moving till things do make sense.

You should keep a notebook with your shipping/receiving information. I think it's better than a cell phone. It also comes in handy if you have to go back in time for information from the past. It's great if your dispatcher tells you to head for a city or area, but he doesn't have an address just yet. You can use your notebook to get moving in the right direction. It's a nice tool to have to help you out. Let's talk about signs. They are definitely there for a reason. Some examples are Low Bridge, No Trucks Left Lane, Speed Limits, High Water, Chains Required, Amish Wagons, and whatever else they have posted. Different states have different rules to the road. Be aware of where you are because when the state trooper has you pulled over, he will not want to listen to your story about how you did not realize that rule. He will be busy writing out your ticket!

Here are a few winter driving tips. Try to keep your fuel tanks half-full. It's not good to run your fuel level low in cold temperatures. I always add winter additive when the temperature gets to be about fifteen degrees. One bottle per tank. Stay on level ground when parking for the night. I try not to set my trailer brakes when I park for the night. They can freeze up. That's why it's good to park on level ground. Carry a small bag of salt, shovel, tire socks, or chains. GOAL. Parking in the dark is a great time to make a mistake. GOAL. Be prepared! Good luck!

CHAPTER 8

PROBLEMS

Problems are definitely a part of the trucking industry. It's not a question if you're going to have a problem. It's when are you going to have a problem. You will have problems. Trucks are big dumb animals. Remember that!

Make sure you are checking your truck out every day and anytime you're sitting around waiting on anything. Carry enough hand tools along so you can deal with small problems. I understand that everybody is not a mechanic, but every driver should carry tools.

Calling the shop to get road service is never fun, so if you can somehow get your truck to the mechanic, that's always a better situation than dealing with it on the highway. Don't be a hero; if you have to make the call, then make the call.

Weather is a major problem. Every driver has a different tolerance level for Mother Nature. Mother Nature will always rule. You will be driving in and out of different types of weather patterns all the time. I myself personally feel that if it's getting out of hand on the highway for whatever reason, I will wait that weather out. Better safe than sorry. Make sure you call your dispatcher and tell them your situation. Nobody will question you about bad weather. If they do try to push you to keep rolling, consider working for another trucking company. Stay safe, and stay alive!

Let's talk about specific weather problems. Snow and ice storms are very dangerous. Telltale signs that things are getting slippery are temperature, ice starting to build up on your mirrors, not the glass, your actual mirror housings, you stop seeing road spray coming off your back tandems and spray coming off of other trucks going the other way, and your tachometer starts racing, which means your drive tires are spinning. When these things start to happen, it's time to slow down and start thinking about shutting your truck down. Remember that this is a marathon, not a sprint. Stay safe!

Rain can also become a bad situation. Springtime rains can lead to flooding. Be aware of your high-water signs in spring.

Wind can be very dangerous. If you are hauling a dry van or a reefer, you should always slow down to whatever speed you are comfortable with. The lighter your truck is, the worse it will be. Straight line winds can flip you over. Don't be a hero!

Fog is another problem. The unknown is very stressful. Slow it down or shut it down. The bottom line is when it comes to weather related problems, you should know your limits. Don't worry about what the rest of the world is doing. If you live by that rule, you should be fine. Live to drive another day!

The classic wrong turn can be a problem. I once made a wrong turn in upper New York State, and it took me an hour to find a place to turn around. *Ouch*! Things do happen while you're out on the road. If you do get offtrack, call your dispatcher and let them know your situation.

Construction and detours can be a problem, but that's why you should start earlier so you can deal with those situations and still be on time.

Parking for the night is always interesting. Try not to park your truck in secluded places. This makes you a target for bad things to happen. Always try to park around a few other trucks. There is safety in numbers. Be aware of your surroundings. Things change from the time you go to bed to the time when you wake up. There are days when I wake up and say, "How the heck am I going to get out of here?"

That's a good time to slow your thinking down and get out and look. This is where you can do damage to your truck, trying to get back on the highway. Remember, trucks are coming and leaving constantly; nothing stays the same for too long.

I'm not a big fan of ramp parking. I will only do it when I absolutely have to. It's dangerous, and you don't have a clue what's going on while you're sleeping. Quite a few states won't let trucks use ramps, period.

Every truck driver should do a daily pre-trip inspection of their truck. Depending on your situation, like where you are or is it super dark out, you might want to get to a better spot and then get out to check your truck over. There are reasons for this move. Lots of things happen while you're sleeping, and if you do your pre-trip in the dark, you might bump into things like varmints, snakes, bad guys, potholes—you name it. It's a long walk to the back of that truck.

You will be traveling to many different places. There will be times when things are great and times where you just kind of land for the night because of your situation. There are places that are not wonderful, but it is part of the job. Truck stops, travel plazas, and gas stations don't just attract truck drivers. They attract all kinds of people. Some of those people have different lifestyles from yours. Always be aware of your situation.

CHAPTER 9

STRESS

Let's talk for a bit about stress. It comes in many forms on this job. The stress of the unknown can be very hard on a person. Being a truck driver is exactly that. You do not have a normal lifestyle. Every day is a different situation with different problems.

You will make many decisions all day, every day. The difference between you and people working more normal jobs is that you are driving a very large vehicle. That's why you must always be thinking ahead. I always try to take the day as it comes to me. I always make sure I'm aware of my time. Being on time is a critical part of the job. It's not easy driving a load of freight, let's say, 1,600 miles, and getting it there on time. You don't want to become the driver that's always late. Your dispatcher won't trust you, and your paycheck will suffer.

Weather is a huge stress problem. The stress of the unknown can wear you out very quickly. Everyone has a different threshold for the weather. Don't be a hero!

Being at your destination can be stressful. Okay! So you are there and on time. Now you have to back into their dock. Oh yeah, there are also ten truck drivers watching your every move. Might be a little bit of stress in that situation. You need to slow down and put that truck in that dock. Remember, GOAL.

America is a large country. But if you run a dedication route, you will get familiar with your job, and you will get comfortable with where to fuel, bunk, shower, and eat. But if you are trucking all over the place, your lifestyle will be very different.

That's why if you have some idea where to fuel, bunk, shower, and eat before you start your day, you don't have to deal with all that stress, and you can concentrate on driving your truck. If I'm not sure what the plan is, I get out my big atlas and try to get a game plan as to where I might end up. Then you can start using your trucker guide and personal guide to get yourself parked for the night.

Big cities are very stressful. Every time you get into a large city, the stress goes sky-high. The chances for bad things to happen explode. The more people, the more problems. I always back off in big cities. The farther, the better within reason. They don't know any better. I've been cut off a million times. I just consider it part of the job.

Most big-city truck stops are pretty nasty. If possible, try to park away from them. All you can do in big cities is go with the flow and get through them.

There will be days when it seems like everything is going wrong. Example: You go to pick your load and end up sitting for five hours at the shipper. The whole time you sit there, you are watching your time slip away. You're somewhere you are not familiar with, and it's going to get dark soon. Your stress level is rising, and it should because this situation drives me nuts! This is where things get tough! You are definitely in a tough spot. I will usually look for a small place to park the truck. Especially if I'm running out of time. The truck stops are usually a mess when you really need one.

Rest areas can get pretty crazy. My last choice would be an on-off ramp. Get out your trucker's guide and do the best you can.

Other stressful situations include "Where will I park for the night? I'm low on fuel, my time clock is running low, am I on time? I need to take the doggie, scale houses, and I forgot about the time zone." The bottom line is that you will be dealing with these problems every day. At first, it will be difficult. As time goes by, it will get better. The stress is always there; it comes down to you. You control how it affects you. That's why a lot of folks try this for a while and end up doing something else for a living. I personally love the freedom and doing and seeing a lot of things most folks only think about. 'Nough said!

CHAPTER 10

TRAILERS

Trailers are another category all their own. Most of the time, things will go well. You must remember that a lot of people are using that trailer. Always do a solid check of that trailer before you start your journey. If you see problems, take some pictures and send them to your dispatcher. The usual problems are flat tires, missing mudflaps, the trailer is scratched or dented, and lights don't work. There are drivers that will pass that trailer and its problems onto the next driver instead of getting it fixed. That kind of stuff is unacceptable.

Make sure you give that trailer a good sweep before you get to your destination. Many places won't load you if the trailer is dirty.

If you do clean a trailer up at a client, sweep it down and put the garbage into a bag, and take it with you. Do not use their parking lot for a garbage can. Never do that!

After I get loaded, I put my personal lock on the backdoor. Sometimes they will lock the load themselves. Remember, that load belongs to you till you get that load to the client.

If you unhook from a trailer to bobtail someplace and plan on coming back later to pick it up, make sure you look the front end of that trailer up. People steal trailers. These things do happen. That's a call you do not want to make to the office. I personally never unhook from a loaded trailer. That load is yours until you get unloaded. If, for some reason, you choose to do that, make sure both ends of that trailer are locked down.

In the winter months, I try not to use my tailer brakes when I'm done driving for the day. They can freeze up on you. Try to park on level ground and just use your tractor brakes. If your trailer brakes do freeze up, you can either loosen them up with your two-pound hammer by banging on them from underneath the trailer or make the service call to have someone come and get you rolling again. Sometimes the slider pins on your trailer will get stuck. Use your hammer to tap them so they will move. The hammer is great for checking your trailer tires to make sure they aren't flat.

CHAPTER 11

THE DEPARTMENT OF TRANSPORTATION

The Department of Transportation is going to be a large part of your world. You do your pre-trip and post-trip inspections for a reason. The first reason is to make sure your truck and trailer are safe to take out on the highway. The second reason is to make sure the DOT people are happy. The last thing you need is to get involved with them. They have the power to inspect your truck whenever they want. Usually it's at the scale houses. *But* they also do random inspections on the highway. Your truck weight is usually what they are interested in, but you just never know what is going to happen at the scale house.

Let's talk about truck weight. In America, a tractor trailer semi-truck can carry a maximum weight of eighty thousand pounds. There are three sets of axles. The steer axle carries twelve thousand pounds. The drive axles carry thirty-four thousand pounds. The rear axles carry thirty-four thousand pounds. This is maximum weight for each set of axles. There is a little wiggle room for the axles. Each set of axles gets about five-hundred-pound wiggle room. Loads under thirty-five thousand pounds really don't need to go to the certified scale. Loads over thirty-five thousand pounds should be scaled.

Keep in mind that just because you just got loaded and your bill of lading says you have thirty-eight thousand pounds on your trailer, it will be just like your last thirty-eight-thousand-pound load. Maybe not! It depends on the load and how they loaded the trailer. All loads are different.

This is why you scale the load. I haul reefer and dry vans. They have adjustable hole-sliding systems so you can move the trailer to get your weight correct. Every truck is a little different when it comes to adjusting load weight. I personally like to start in the no. 10 hole on my truck set up. That usually gets my truck fairly close to being legal right away. Generally speaking, the axle weight will move about four hundred pounds for every hole in the slide. But like I said, every load is different. Heavy loads are tricky sometimes, and you might have trouble sliding your trailer. When this happens, I try to get my trailer on a slight incline so gravity will help it move. Just a tip!

Most scale houses will be located at the state borders. Larger states will have scale houses within the state.

Your Rand McNally Road Atlas has a complete breakdown on where every scale house is located for every state.

The atlas also has a listing for every low bridge in every state. The atlas is a very good tool for you to use as a reference.

Keep your truck information in an easy place to find in case you do get inspected at the scale house. Keep up with your logbook because they are the law.

You should carry safety equipment. A neon vest, safety glasses, hard hat, work boots, and a pair of pants. Some places won't let you enter the facility unless you're wearing pants and closed shoes. No shorts and no sandals. Be prepared.

CHAPTER 12

TOOL LIST

Cab Tools

- Rand McNally Road Atlas
- Truck GPS Unit
- CB Radio
- Big Calendar—Yearly Information
- Pocket Truck Stop Guide
- Notebook to write down delivery information

- Small Notebook, as a personal journal
- Microwave Oven
- Medical Kit—Tooth pain, eye drops, etc.

Truck Tools

- Good Push Broom
- Two-Pound or Three-Pound Hammer
- Air Gauge
- Flashlight
- Extra Headlight, Wiper, Blades, Fuses, and Fifth Wheel Lube
- Correct Oil, Antifreeze, and Window Wash
- Big funnel, Rags, Paper towels, and Glass Cleaner
- Glad Hand Seals

- Two-Load Straps and Two-Load Bars
- Trailer Locks, front and back
- Bungee Chords
- Miscellaneous Hand Tools

ABOUT THE AUTHOR

Bruce DAngelo is an old school father of three great kids. Likes to cook, hunt, fish, and play with large trucks!! He has a really big soft spot for doggies & kitty cats!!! The author just loves life!!